Exploring
African-American
Culture
Through Crafts

Mia Farrell

 Enslow Publishing
101 W. 23rd Street
Suite 240
New York, NY 10011
USA

enslow.com

Published in 2016 by Enslow Publishing, LLC.
101 W. 23rd Street, Suite 240, New York, NY 10011

Cataloging-in-Publication Data
Farrell, Mia.
Exploring African-American culture through crafts / by Mia Farrell.
p. cm. — (Multicultural crafts)
Includes bibliographical references and index.
ISBN 978-0-7660-6771-4 (library binding)
ISBN 978-0-7660-6769-1 (pbk.)
ISBN 978-0-7660-6770-7 (6-pack)
1. Handicraft —Juvenile literature. 2. African Americans in art — Juvenile literature. I. Title.
TT160.F377 2016
745.5089'96073—d23

Printed in the United States of America

To Our Readers: We have done our best to make sure all Web site addresses in this book were active and appropriate when we went to press. However, the author and the publisher have no control over and assume no liability for the material available on those Web sites or on any Web sites they may link to. Any comments or suggestions can be sent by e-mail to customerservice@enslow.com.

Portions of this book originally appeared in the book *African-American Crafts Kids Can Do!* by Carol Gnojewski.

Photo Credits: Crafts prepared by June Ponte; craft photography by Lindsay Pries. Andra Simionescu/Digital Vision Vectors/Getty Images (background throughout book); Anthony Barboza/Archive Photos/Getty Images, p. 14; Ben Martin/The LIFE Images Collection/Getty Images, p. 16; Emaonn McCabe/Redferns/Getty Images, p. 18; Gregory Johnston/Shutterstock.com, p. 24; Hulton Archive/Archive Photos/Getty Images, p. 12; John W Banagan/Stone/ Getty Images, p. 20; li jianbing /Shutterstock.com, p. 10; mileswork/Shutterstock.com, p. 1 (Earth icon); Science & Society Picture Library/SSPL/Getty Images, p. 8; Stock Montage/Archive Photos/Getty Images, p. 4; SuperStock/ Getty Images, p. 22; Traveller Martin/Shutterstock.com, p. 6; William Lovelace/Express/Hulton Archive/Getty Images, p. 5.

Cover Credits: Crafts prepared by June Ponte; craft photography by Lindsay Pries. Andra Simionescu/Digital Vision Vectors/Getty Images (background); mileswork/Shutterstock.com (Earth icon).

CONTENTS

Safety Note: *Be sure to ask for help from an adult, if needed, to complete these crafts!*

African-American History and Art

African Americans have had a centuries-long struggle for freedom and equality. Africans were brought to the United States as slaves, where they struggled against inhumane living and working conditions, as well as new diseases, languages, and other hardships.

Though the Civil War (1861–1865) fought to end slavery, conditions for blacks did not improve. Abolitionists and leaders began to emerge, such as Frederick Douglass, who escaped from slavery and became a statesman, and Harriet Tubman, whose courage and bravery led more than three hundred people to freedom on the Underground Railroad.

In the 1920s, an artistic and creative movement

Frederick Douglass

On March 30, 1965, Martin Luther King Jr. (front center) led a voting rights march from Selma, Alabama, to Montgomery, the state capital.

emerged in New York City. The Harlem Renaissance gave the world great African-American writers, artists, and musicians who would forever change the culture of the United States.

The 1950s brought about a movement for civil rights. Women, blacks, and other minorities fought for equal rights. People like Rosa Parks and Martin Luther King Jr. peacefully protested inequality, speaking out against injustice, and inspiring a generation of Americans.

Each of the crafts in this book tells a little bit about African-American culture and history. Some of the people mentioned here are famous, some are less known. But each of these crafts will inform and inspire you to learn more about the rich African-American culture.

STAR PUZZLE

INSPIRED BY BENJAMIN BANNEKER

Benjamin Banneker (1731–1806) was a colonial farmer and almanac writer who had a talent for math. He made predictions about the weather by looking at the stars, and he enjoyed creating and solving puzzles. Make your own star puzzle like Benjamin Banneker.

Benjamin Banneker used the stars to predict tides and eclipses.

WHAT YOU WILL NEED

- yellow and blue craft foam
- pen
- scissors
- glue
- cardboard
- glitter (optional)
- star stickers (optional)
- permanent marker

1. Using the pattern on page 27, trace a star onto yellow craft foam and carefully cut it out.

2. Trace the yellow star onto a piece of blue craft foam. Cut out the blue star. Glue the blue craft foam onto a piece of cardboard. Decorate the blue craft foam with glitter and star stickers.

3. With a permanent marker, trace the outline of the star on the cardboard. This is now your puzzle board. Use a pen to divide the yellow star into various shapes to form puzzle pieces. Cut out each piece.

4. Trace the pieces onto the cardboard puzzle. Number the backs of the puzzle pieces and the puzzle board with permanent marker so that the puzzle is easier to complete later.

LIGHT BRIGHT DESIGN

INSPIRED BY LEWIS LATIMER

Lewis Latimer (1848–1928), inventor and engineer, worked with some of the most famous inventors of his time, including Alexander Graham Bell (1847–1922) and Thomas Edison (1847–1931). In 1881, Latimer patented a process for making carbon filaments in lightbulbs. Be inspired by Latimer and make your own light bright design.

These are what lightbulbs looked like in Latimer's time.

WHAT YOU WILL NEED

- black and yellow construction paper
- scissors
- hole punch
- glue
- index card
- white reinforcement circles
- crayons or markers

1. Cut two 4 x 6-inch (10 x 15 cm) rectangles out of construction paper, one black and one yellow.

2. Use the hole punch to evenly punch holes in the black rectangle to make a grid. Make eight holes down and twelve holes across. Space the holes 1/4 inch (1/3 cm) apart. There should be ninety-six holes in all. Glue the black grid onto the yellow paper.

3. On an index card, make your own design: a flower, a boat, an emoji, or whatever else you'd like. Decide how many reinforcement circles you will need to make that design on the grid. Use crayons or markers to color the reinforcement circles as you'd like.

4. Arrange the reinforcement circles on the grid by placing them over the punched holes. The circles may overlap each other. The yellow paper will make your design looks as if it's glowing!

9

Peanut Planters

Inspired by George Washington Carver

George Washington Carver (1864–1943) worked to educate farmers about how to keep the soil healthy for planting. He was an educator and botanist who experimented with new uses for crops, such as dyes and adhesives. His research helped make peanut butter popular. Here's a creative use for peanut shells that Carver would be proud of!

Peanuts grow underground. They are good for you and have many uses.

What You Will Need

- whole peanuts in the shell
- poster paint
- paintbrushes
- colored sand
- herb or cactus seeds
- plant mister

*** If you are allergic to peanuts, please do not do this craft.

1. Carefully split peanut shells in half lengthwise and remove the peanuts.

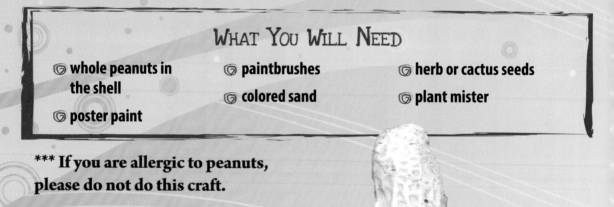

2. Paint the shells bright colors using poster paint. Let dry.

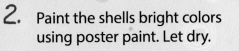

3. Fill the shell halves with colored sand. Add a few herb or cactus seeds to each shell half and cover with more sand.

5. After they've sprouted, place the planters directly into the soil of a pot or garden.

4. Use a plant mister to moisten the sand. Place the planters in a sunny window and watch as your seeds begin to sprout!

3-D Stunt Spinner

Inspired by the Harlem Globetrotters

In the 1920s, Harlem, New York, was considered the cultural center for African Americans. In 1926, the Harlem Globetrotters began as a basketball team in Chicago. The reference to Harlem let basketball fans know that the Globetrotters were an all-black team. In 1939, the Globetrotters added comedy and stunts to their game, something the team still performs today. Make your own 3-D stunt spinner inspired by the Harlem Globetrotters!

Harlem Globetrotters practice their stunt spinning.

What You Will Need

- white paper
- paper plate
- scissors
- basketball
- orange crayon or colored pencil
- glue
- hole punch
- yarn or string

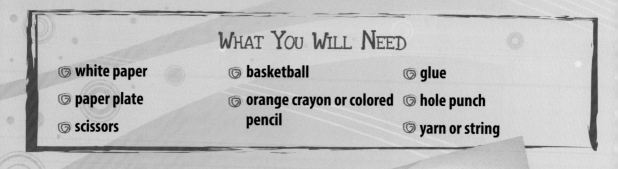

1. Use either a paper plate or the pattern on page 26 to trace eight circles onto white paper. Cut out the circles.

2. Using an orange crayon or colored pencil, make rubbings of a basketball on both sides of each paper circle.

3. Fold each circle into quarters and re-open. Cut along one fold to the center of the circle. Fold one cut quarter over the other and glue in place. The circle should now have three sides. Do this to the rest of the circles.

4. Glue four of these triangular pieces together so that they form a half-circle. Do the same with the other four. You should have two half- circles this way.

5. Glue the flat bottom of one half-circle to the other. This will create a full circle.

6. Use a hole punch to create a hole in the top of the spinner, and thread yarn or ribbon through it. Now your basketball is ready to spin!

Neighborhood Collage

Inspired by Romare Bearden

Romare Bearden (1911–1988) was a painter and songwriter in Harlem. During the 1960s, he developed a unique collage technique using images of African Americans from magazines and newspapers and arranging, layering, and drawing on them. You can show off your community by creating your own collage.

Bearden's artwork focused on African-American life.

What You Will Need

- magazines (ask permission first!)
- scissors
- pencil
- construction paper
- ruler
- glue
- crayons or markers

1. Go through the magazines and cut out any images that you like and those that remind you of your neighborhood.

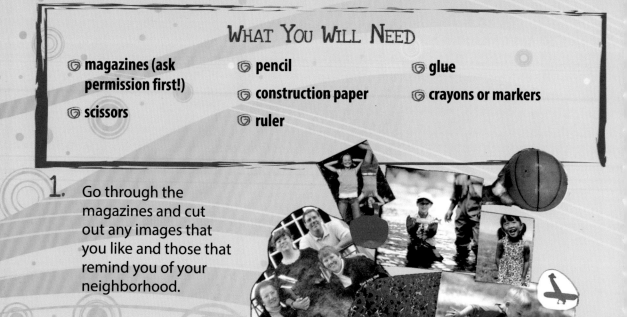

2. Draw an outline of your home on a piece of construction paper with a ruler. Leave room for a sidewalk, yard, or street.

3. Draw the windows and doors of your house onto a separate piece of construction paper. Cut out these windows and doors.

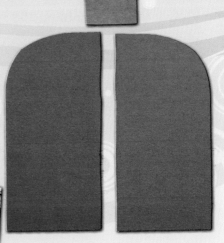

4. Glue the images you cut from the magazines inside the windows and on the sidewalks, yard, or street of your home. The images do not have to fit the spaces, or be realistic. Use crayons and markers to add texture such as brick on buildings. Cut images into the shapes of things you need. For example, a picture of a person could be cut into a curtain for a window. A flower could be a chimney. A vegetable could be a car. There is no wrong way to make a collage!

INVISIBLE MESSAGE

INSPIRED BY RALPH ELLISON

Ralph Ellison (1914–1994) shared what it was like to be African American through stories, poems, and essays. In 1953, Ralph Ellison won the National Book Award for his first novel, Invisible Man. Make your own symbols to create an invisible message for a friend.

Ralph Ellison was inspired by the music, literature, and art of his day.

WHAT YOU WILL NEED

- 5 x 8-inch (12 x 20 cm) index cards
- white crayon
- pen or pencil
- black poster paint
- paintbruth
- water

1. Using a white crayon, draw your own symbols, words, or designs onto the blank side on an index card.

Dear Lori,
My message says:

"YOU ARE THE APPLE OF MY EYE!"

From, Lisa

2. Write a short note to a friend on the lined side of the card.

Dear Lori,
My message says:

"YOU ARE THE APPLE OF MY EYE!"

From, Lisa

TO: Lori Smith
123 Main St.
NEWTON, NJ
00050   USA

From: Lisa Jones
345 South St.
Newton, NJ
00050

3. Ask your friend to make a black wash by thinning black poster paint (two parts paint to one part water). Then, have your friend lightly brush the wash over the front of the index card to reveal your hidden message or design.

4. Once dry, the postcard can be hung up for decoration.

MURABARABA WORD SCRAMBLE

INSPIRED BY RITA DOVE

In 1993, poet Rita Dove (1952–) became the youngest poet laureate of the United States at the age of forty-one, and the first African American to hold this honor. Polish your word skills with this board game, based on a South African strategy game called murabaraba.

Rita Dove has won many awards for her poetry and plays.

WHAT YOU WILL NEED

- cardboard
- poster paint
- paintbrush
- ruler
- markers
- scissors

1. Paint a 12 x 12 inch (30 x 30 cm) piece of cardboard with light-colored poster paint. Let dry. This will be the game board.

2. Use a marker and ruler to draw a large square 1½ inches (4 cm) from the edge of the cardboard. Draw another square 1½ inches (4 cm) inside the first square. Draw another square 1½ inches (4 cm) inside the second one. Repeat this until the cardboard is divided into a total of four squares.

3. Find the center of the cardboard and use a ruler to draw a horizontal and a vertical line through the center. Draw diagonal lines through the middle of the squares so that all the corners are connected.

4. Cut fifty 1-inch (2½ cm) squares out of another piece of cardboard. These will be the game pieces. Paint them and let them dry. Label the pieces as noted on page 29.

5. Play the word scramble following the rules laid out on page 28.

Graffiti Name Tag

Inspired by Fab 5 Freddy

Fab 5 Freddy (Fred Brathewaite) hosted the television show Yo! MTV Raps and helped introduce hip-hop to the word. Freddy was also a street artist and performer who helped bring urban culture to the masses.

These tags represent several different graffiti artists.

Personal identity is a big part of hip-hop and graffiti culture. Graffiti artists in the 1970s signed, or tagged, their art. Sometimes the tag itself was the art. A tag was a nickname and a number, usually the street number where the artist lived. Show off your identity with this graffiti name tag.

What You Will Need

- newspaper
- sidewalk chalk
- water
- bowl
- brown paper bag
- scissors
- markers

1. Cover your workspace with newspaper. Place sidewalk chalk in a bowl of water. Let the chalk moisten.

2. Cut a brown paper bag down the seams. Place the bag blank side up. Think of a "tag" that includes a number that has some significance. It could be your birthday. Your street number. Or even part of a phone number.

3. Use markers to draw the outline of your "tag." Make it large enough to fill the paper.

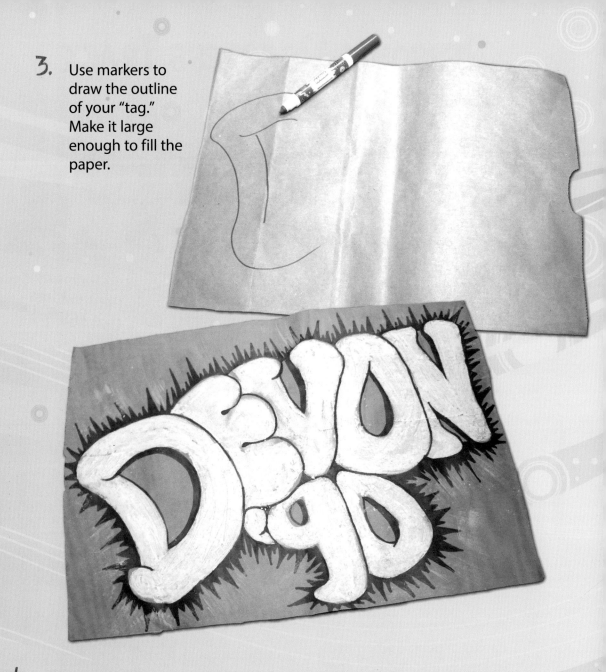

4. Fill in your "tag" with sidewalk chalk. The wet chalk will have a creamy, paste-like texture. Apply it thickly. When it's dry, the wet chalk with have an airbrushed or spray-painted effect.

Personal Progress Track

Inspired by Harriet Tubman

Harriet Tubman (1820–1913) escaped a life of slavery in the South with the help of abolitionists. Inspired to help others in the same way, Tubman helped hundreds of slaves escape to the North by an escape route called the Underground Railroad. It was a series of secret hiding places such as barns, tunnels, and woods.

The Underground Railroad was a network that stretched from the Southern United States into Canada.

Make your own railroad track to show the progress you've made in your life.

What You Will Need

- craft sticks
- markers
- 2 dowels or sticks
- poster paint (optional)
- glue

---

1. On the craft sticks, write the names of people who have helped or inspired you, special events, or some of your personal goals.

MOM+DAD

PILOT

DOG TRAINER

2. Place two dowels vertically so that they are parallel to each other. Paint them if you wish. Let dry.

ASTRONAUT

DOG TRAINER

PILOT

SCHOOL

MOM & DAD

3. Place the craft sticks in order, starting at the bottom with the events that happened first. Place the most recent events and your goals at the top. Glue the craft sticks onto the dowels like railroad tracks. Let dry.

EQUATION BRACELET

INSPIRED BY BOB MOSES

Bob Moses (1935–) is a philosopher, mathematician, educator, and activist. He took part in the civil rights movement during the 1960s and later founded the Algebra Project, which helps students learn math. Use your math skills to make a bead bracelet.

$$\frac{1}{3}x = 2$$
$$3(\tfrac{1}{3}x) = 3(2)$$
$$x = 6$$

Algebra is just one of the many kinds of maths children learn in school.

WHAT YOU WILL NEED

- paper
- pencil
- yarn or ribbon
- scissors
- beads

---

1. Write the following algebra property on paper: a + b = b + a. This equation is called the additive commutative property.

2. Cut a 10-inch (25½ cm) length of yarn or ribbon and find the center of the yarn.

3. Make a color pattern for your bracelet using this equation. For example, if "a" stands for yellow, "b" would stand for a different color, like red.

4. Decide how many beads of each color you would like to have on the bracelet. You might decide to have 6 yellow (a) beads and 5 red (b) beads. Rewrite the equation to match. This equation would read: 6a + 5b = 5b + 6a.

PATTERNS

The percentages included on the patterns tell you how much to enlarge or shrink the image using a copier. Most copiers and printers have an adjustable size/percentage feature to change the size of an image when you print it. After you print the pattern to its correct size, cut it out. Trace it onto the material listed in the craft.

3-D Globetrotter Stunt Spinner

At 100%

Star Puzzle

Enlarge by 123%

Game Rules

Murabaraba Word Scramble
Inspired by Rita Dove

1. Play with up to four players. Turn over game pieces so that the letters do not show.

2. Each player will select five pieces at a time.

3. Words must be laid down on the triangles and can run forwards, backwards, diagonal, and across.

4. After each play, take more pieces so that you always have five at any given time.

5. Play until the game board is filled or you cannot make any more words.

LETTER	NUMBER OF PIECES	LETTER	NUMBER OF PIECES
e	3	f	2
t	3	p	2
a	3	b	2
i	3	u	1
s	3	g	1
o	3	w	1
n	3	y	1
r	3	v	1
h	2	k	1
d	2	j	1
l	2	q	1
c	2	x	1
m	2	z	1

LEARN MORE

Abdul-Jabbar, Kareem, Raymond Obstfeld, and Ben Boos. *What Color Is My World?: The Lost History of African-American Inventors.* Somerville, Mass.: Candlewick Press, 2012.

Lassieur, Allison, Robert L. McConnel, and Timothy, J. Griffin. *The Harlem Renaissance.* North Mankato, Minn.: Capstone Press, 2014.

Roessel, David. *Poetry for Young People: Langston Hughes.* New York: Sterling Children's Books, 2013.

Saunders, Nancy L. *Frederick Douglass for Kids: His Life and Times, with 21 Activities.* Chicago: Chicago Review Press, 2012.

WEB SITES

dltk-kids.com/crafts/black_history_month.htm

Check out ideas for crafts inspired by Black History Month.

teacher.scholastic.com/activities/bhistory/underground_ railroad/harriet_tubman.htm

Learn more about Harriet Tubman's life and the Underground Railroad.

teacher.scholastic.com/activities/bhistory.

Learn more about African-American history.

INDEX